PEMBROKESHIRE

AND

SOUTH WEST WALES

By

A. G. BRADLEY

Author of

"*Highways and Byways in South Wales*"
"*In Praise of North Wales*"
"*Exmoor Memories*"
"*Round about Wiltshire*"
&c.

GREAT WESTERN RAILWAY COMPANY
[James Milne, General Manager]
Paddington Station, London, W.2
1930

CONTENTS

Chapter

FOREWORD

It is difficult to believe in this Island of ours, that there is still a considerable portion of beautiful territory comparatively unexplored. In Pembrokeshire, with its "Little England beyond Wales," and South West Wales generally, Mr. A. G. Bradley, the well-known travel writer, has again returned to a favourite subject of his, and it is hoped that more travellers will be induced to visit a district which provides so much charm and interest.

NEVERN CHURCH.

St. David's Cathedral : The travel shrine of Pembrokeshire

PEMBROKESHIRE

AND

SOUTH WEST WALES

CHAPTER I

CARMARTHEN,
A CONVENIENT STARTING POINT

EVERY main route, into or out of South-West Wales, goes through Carmarthen. Its situation alone ensures what the custom of ages has followed. Seated on a ridge above the Towy, here meeting the tide, and thence gradually widening towards its estuary, with the castle at one extremity, and its fine monastic church at the other, the old town has no little dignity of pose. And this is only suitable in view of its long history beginning, by repute, with the birth here of Merlin, and showing traces of Roman occupation. The Towy is here spanned by an ancient bridge of seven arches, the last upon the river, and about it may still be seen the coracles of the fishermen, those ancient British craft of tarpaulin stretched on wickerwork. They are used here by salmon netters, while the fish that get past them up the river, together with the indigenous trout, afford good sport to anglers. The towers, which almost alone survive of the ancient fortress, now form the town jail, but are much obscured by modern buildings. This is unfortunate as the castle typifies the ancient strength of the place as a chief stronghold of the Princes of South Wales. A long bloody tale of struggles for its capture or defence by Norman barons, English kings and Welsh princes attaches to old Carmarthen. Over a century after the completed conquest of Wales, 1282, and its subsequent risings in South Wales had terminated all this strife, Glyndwr's insurrection revived it again. That leader was frequently here besieging and capturing and burning the town in 1403, when unknown to him, his new ally Hotspur was expecting his aid at the decisive battle of Shrewsbury, so critical for both England and Wales. Two years later, assisted by a French army, landed at Milford Haven, he re-occupied it with-out resistance. From Carmarthen the allied forces marched via Glamorgan into Worcestershire, only to retreat again before King Henry's pursuing army into south-west Wales, where half the French wintered, to the

CORACLE MAN.

Carmarthen, and River Towy

Coracle men, Carmarthen

discontent both of themselves and their hosts. In the Civil wars Carmarthen was held for the king, but captured by Laugharne the Pembrokeshire parliamentary general.

The chief attraction of the town to-day is St. Peter's church, consisting of a fine 13th century tower and nave with a later south aisle, chapel and north transept. Of its interior monuments the most notable is an altar tomb with recumbent effigies of Sir Rhys ap Thomas and his wife, the greatest soldier and most accomplished gentleman in Wales at Henry the Seventh's accession, as well as the wealthiest. He was foremost among the group that received Henry at Milford, rallied Wales to his standard and fought by his side on Bosworth field. A doubtful tradition credits Sir Rhys with actually killing Richard III. A brass tablet in the south chapel commemorates Sir Richard Steel, the famous man of letters, who married a lady of property in the neighbourhood and died here. A Roman altar in the church porch is one of many relics that prove the Roman occupation. At a spot just east of the church the Protestant bishop Ferrars was burned during the Marian re-action. Two local heroes are honoured by statues in the town. General Nott, who, after winning fame and a knighthood in India, died here, his father being then proprietor of the still much patronised *Ivybush* hotel. A loftier shaft commemorates Sir Charles Picton of Waterloo fame, who was of a Pembrokeshire family. There are other memorials to the fallen in later wars, including, of course, the last and greatest.

Carmarthen is a solid old-fashioned town unremarkable in the main, but with quaint bits in its ancient quarters. It is intensely Welsh, and might be called the capital of south-west Wales. Not because it is rather larger than any other towns in that region (10,000 population), but that it has always been the popular and convenient place of meetings, social, political or clerical, for the three counties. It was the last stronghold of the old Welshwoman's hat which forty to fifty years ago finally disappeared from the Welsh market places. A pleasant upland grass country of high hills and ridges spreads all around it, laced with lush hedgerows and sprinkled with the typical white homesteads and their sheltering groves of ash and sycamore. The valley of the Gwili winding down from the north through wooded gorges and threaded both by the road and railroad running up to Cardiganshire, is most beautiful. While at its mouth, where it joins the Towy near Carmarthen at Abergwili, is the Palace of the Bishops of St. David's. The beautiful vale of Towy is outside our district, save that its charming scenery and admirable fishing, together with that of its equally delectable tributary, the Cothi, can be conveniently covered from Carmarthen, where there are several excellent hotels.

For south-west Wales, however, Carmarthen will probably be regarded by the traveller rather as a convenient base than as a place of great interest in itself. No better view of the tidal portion of the Towy below can be had than from the G.W.R. main line trains. On a sunny summer morning, the verdure of the meadows, the bright coils of the sparkling river between the overhanging hills, makes a charming picture. Finally it expands into a broad sandy estuary, with the castle of Llanstephan crowning a high hill upon the western shore, and that of Kidwelly looking down upon its little borough town on the other. First erected by William de Londres of the Glamorgan conquering group, Kidwelly was re-built in the next century. Besides the fine embattled gateway with many chambers, giving into an outer ward with curtain walls, there is an inner ward protected by round towers. The little river Gwendraeth skirts the steep castle hill, and the massive crumbling towers are often beautifully mirrored on its quiet surface. The 13th century cruciform church of Benedictine foundation with its noble tower and lofty spire—rare object in rural Wales—is conspicuous in the little town.

CHAPTER II

LITTLE ENGLAND BEYOND WALES

ONE looks southward from Kidwelly over immense marshes and tossing sand dunes. But it is westward our course here lies, where over the mingling estuaries of the Towy and the Tâf, forming the centre of Carmarthen bay, one sees the high rugged headlands of the Tenby coast. Across these broad wet sands and flowing tides lies the country known as "Little England beyond Wales." Though the coast belt for a few miles is nowadays Carmarthen territory, it formerly belonged to Pembrokeshire and shares the same strange history.

Now it is impossible to approach Pembrokeshire [by G.W.R. from Carmarthen via Whitland (boundary) to Tenby] without preparing the visitor for conditions that have no parallel elsewhere in Britain. No intelligent traveller could even glance at his map without being struck by the change in place-names which takes place on crossing into south Pembrokeshire. After passing through all Wales, where practically every name is Welsh, he finds himself suddenly in a region where the nomenclature is almost as wholly English as in Hants or Gloucester, not merely for a few parishes, but throughout half

Saundersfoot

Tenby, Castle Hill and Harbour

a county. Most people have heard vaguely of "Little England beyond Wales" but few realise its full significance. It is such a leading feature in south-west Wales, otherwise so intensely Celtic, that I must endeavour to explain the apparent anomaly, in brief, but unavoidably in rather general terms. Now the conquest, or rather partial conquest of Wales by the Normans which with a short interval followed that of England, was on similar lines but with a difference. Speaking broadly, north Wales was conquered gradually by the Crown and held by Norman officials of the King or by Welsh princes, nominally independent but tributary to the Crown.

South Wales, on the other hand, was conquered by Norman barons, with a licence from the Crown to take all that each one of them could, and hold their lands as independent fiefs or lordships, with a nominal allegiance only to the King. A few Welsh chieftains remained under similar conditions. But nowhere were the Welsh people displaced. The Norman barons in their strong castles remained merely overlords, with a limited following of soldiers and dependents. But southern Pembrokeshire was a sharp exception. Partly no doubt as a smooth and fertile region, partly for political reasons, encouraged and even aided by William II and Henry I, the conquerors of southern Pembrokeshire, among whom one Arnulph de Montgomery was foremost, drove the Welsh population by degrees and after much hard fighting clean out into the more mountainous northern portion of the province. The land was then re-settled by colonists from England and Flanders.

The two races, colonists and Welsh, henceforward remained entirely apart in their separate divisions of what became the county of Pembroke. The line between them, running through the middle of the shire, remains as sharp as ever to this day. The northern or Welsh half was conquered after the usual

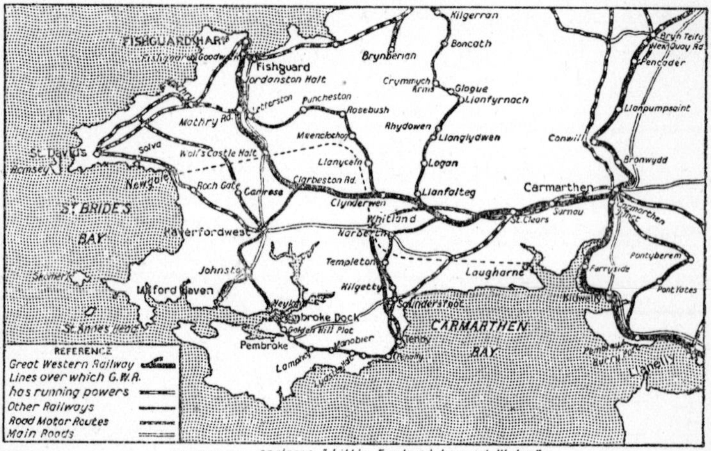

-------- encloses "Little England beyond Wales"

Norman-Welsh fashion by Martin de Tours, but far more mildly than elsewhere. For Martin, landing with a strong force at Fishguard, secured the allegiance of the Welsh chiefs mainly by friendly overtures, and with his heirs exercised a mild and apparently popular overlordship of the resident natives, together with those driven in there from the south ; his followers marrying Welsh wives. Southern Pembrokeshire, in the meantime, in its earlier days received two separate importations of Flemings, one of superfluous mercenaries stranded in England, the other of refugees from inundations in Holland. Both were encouraged

Pembroke, view from the Castle

Pendine Sands

by the Crown as strengthening this outpost of English power in the rear of the ever rebellious and militant Welsh. All this was in the 12th century. Medieval English and Flemings mingled easily in their isolation in front of a common enemy, and in time merged into a homogeneous English-speaking community.

Pembroke was kept as an outpost of the Crown under its Earls as the King's representative. The northern or Welsh half of it, though remaining a fief of the Martin de Tours family, with a further slice under the Bishop of St. David's, in course of time, though not without sharing in the occasional attacks of the up-country Welsh princes on the Anglo-Flemish colony, fell automatically into line with the County Palatine of Pembroke. But for all future ages and with little bloodshed between them, the two races, different in blood, traditions and speech, held fast to their own territories, regarding each other as Welsh and English respectively and never mixing or inter-marrying across the boundary. If this sharp cleavage has lost a little force in the last generation or two, what does this amount to in eight centuries? But the rooted prejudices (hardly enmities) of eight centuries in voice and speech are prodigious and beyond the comprehension of normal English folk in Hampshire or Norfolk. Such in brief is this "Little England beyond Wales." Yet Pembrokeshire as a "Welsh" and "English" county is as united and proud of itself as any in Wales, which seems anomalous but is nevertheless true. There is nothing unfriendly in this strange cleavage. It is too ancient and matter of fact for that. Immigrants from other regions have come into both sections from all parts through the ages, as with all seaboard counties, though mostly into south Pembrokeshire. But that makes no difference. They have been assimilated by each community. I need hardly add that these conditions do not apply to the higher classes. Nor, of course, is it implied that Pembrokeshire Welshmen are not to be found scattered about in English Pembrokeshire, though the reverse is less common. Just as they are met with in Shropshire or Herefordshire—save here that they are in their own county though in an alien district. It is all very anomalous to be sure, and as already stated has no counterpart in Britain.

CHAPTER III

SOUTH PEMBROKESHIRE

GOING " down the line," as the local saying has it, by the G.W.R. from Carmarthen to Tenby, Whitland Junction with its Town marks the county boundary. Lines run thence to Haverfordwest, two separate ones to Fishguard and yet another, most beautiful of all, to Cardigan. When you have traversed them all with a reasonably observant eye, in addition to a few short trips by rail, or road in the Western Welsh Company's motors, you will have obtained a fairly good picture of this always pleasing and often beautiful county. At Whitland the river Tâf comes down from the distant Precelly mountains and runs out at Laugharne as an estuary into Carmarthen bay. Laugharne is itself well worth visiting (station St. Clears) or by 'bus from Carmarthen (12 miles). A small borough under a portreeve and jury and cherishing many quaint old customs, it also possesses a Norman castle, of which a gateway with drum towers, a keep and fragments of other buildings survive. It was built by Guy de Brian in the 13th century on the site of a former structure. Along its seacoast marsh run the famous Pendine sands notable as the scene of National motor speed trials. Eastward across the river mouth rises the high block, from the further side of which the castle of Llanstephen and its picturesque village looks across the mouth of the Towy. Built by the Norman-Glamorgan buccaneer de Londres, there remains of it the gatehouse, a rectangular keep and some curtain walls. Its site is a noble one, so is the view from it. The village itself is charming and has an interesting cruciform church. Near Whitland, the slender remains of a Cistercian abbey, endowed by Welsh princes, stand on the river bank a mile from the station. Here, too, the great law-making Prince Howel Dda in the 10th century met his national assembly and drew up the famous and curious code of laws for Wales, known by his name and to be read in print to-day. The line on to Tenby runs through broken and picturesque country ; deep woody dingles wind between lofty hills to the sea, while occasionally wide prospects open out into the grassy heart of south Pembrokeshire. The station of Saundersfoot gives a two-mile walk down a profusely wooded valley to that charming little resort with its beautiful sandy bay and small harbour nestling between high rocky promontories.

Taken all round, Tenby is one of the most attractive watering places in the kingdom, and yet how comparatively few know it! Lifted up in an angle, ending in a rugged promontory carrying a ruined castle, it possesses two separate and beautiful bays, facing north and south respectively. The former is bordered by the old town, with its interesting harbour filled with craft, its curving sandy shore, and vista of high bold headlands and islands spreading away to Saundersfoot and Laugharne, and terminating with the lofty and distant promontory of Gower, running far seaward to the fantastic headland of the "Worm." On the outstanding point parting the north and south bay are the remains of the castle, and beyond that again the high, rocky little islet, accessible at low tide, of St. Catherine, carrying what was once a fort. High medieval walls, with round towers at intervals run from the castle promontory right through the town, dividing the older historic Tenby from the newer watering place. The former is full of handsome old houses and quaint buildings. The latter, built when Tenby became a seaside resort is more comely than most such places and eminently bright and cheerful. This modern town, with its fine parade, looks out on to the south bay with its mile long curving sweep of the finest sands imaginable. These terminate in the rugged cliffs and bold headland of Giltar. From this again stretches out to sea a protecting barrier against south-west storms for two miles, the linked islands of St. Margaret, mere rocks, and Caldy, fertile but hilly and cliff girt. Till the Dissolution Caldy was occupied by Benedictine monks: their ancient priory church still remains, together with a 6th century Ogham stone. After varying fortunes, it is now again occupied and owned by Benedictine monks, in this case from Belgium. A long stretch of sand dunes behind the south bay give character to a golf course of old-standing and first class quality, while there is also excellent boating and sea fishing, and I need hardly add bathing. For the naturalist and geologist, too, Tenby has peculiar interest, the cliff formations of the carboniferous limestone interspersed with old red sandstone and Silurian rock being often of the weirdest kind. The flora for similar reasons has a wide and varied range, while for sea birds the coast has among ornithologists a national reputation. Tenby is quite unique in possessing these two beautiful bays facing in opposite directions within a few minutes walk of each other. Nor is there another seaside resort nor any other town in Britain, save Conway, showing such a fine display of perfect medieval walls and towers breathing so eloquently of sieges and battles long ago. For those who like a definite centre, Tenby with its wide choice of accommodation is much the best point from which to explore south Pembrokeshire. The good service of trains and motor 'buses are available for the many who depend on public conveyances. The air is fresh, with prevailing winds from the west or south-west, but the climate is of the mild type in winter, common to the coasts of south-west Britain. Just west of Tenby comes the beautiful bay of Lydstep, with beetling, cavernous cliffs forming both of its grim, wavebeaten horns, and a wealth of woodland sloping down to the curving sands embayed between them. The whole prospect bursting suddenly on the visitor is glorious. And round the high headlands westward is Manorbier, another bay, beautiful too in a rather different fashion. For here green meadowy upward slopes crowned by a picturesque village, with an outstanding castle fill a narrower bay, between two high rocky headlands.

Llanstephan Castle

Tenby, St. Catherine's Rock

Of the castle one may only say here that it is considered one of the best existing specimens of a Norman baron's fortress residence; that it was originally built by Gerald de Windsor, Henry the First's Constable at Pembroke, the husband of the beautiful south Welsh Princess Nesta, the "Helen of Wales," and the birthplace (1146) of their immortal grandson Giraldus Cambrensis, cleric, chronicler, politician, humorist. Most of the present building dates from the 13th century. A trifling fee admits the visitor over the drawbridge and through the noble embattled gateway into the beautiful quadrangular court, surrounded by crenelated curtain walls and flanked by many of the still surviving buildings. An unobtrusive private residence just under the gateway accounts in part for the charming garden-like interior of the great court. Across the little valley down which a stream, which once filled large fishponds, plashes to the sea, stands a typical old Pembrokeshire church. Its rather slender, lofty embattled tower gives the body below, of two gabled aisles and a transept, the slightly dwarfed appearance characteristic of the country. The way in which the Norman interior was converted into Early English, however, is peculiarly quaint and unusual. On the hill above is a well-known cromlech. In the horns of the little bay, the carboniferous limestone giving way for a space to warm red sandstone, glows most effectively under a bright sun and against a blue sea. A day at Manorbier either by 'bus direct or train (station 1 mile) is an indispensable feature of a Tenby visit.

The length of coastline hence to the wide mouth of Milford Haven is about 25 miles and for the greater part high and rugged. For those unprepared to walk along the cliffs, generally good going, the most profitable and accessible points of approach on wheels are the Stack rocks near Flimston and St. Govans Head near Bosherston, some four miles

STACK ROCKS.

apart. From both a fine vista of cliff scenery in two directions is displayed, while each shows at and around it as striking examples of this grand coast formation as could be gained. For miles along the sheer cliff edges stretch level open pasture lands, admitting ready access by good farm lanes to motors of any kind. The Stack Rocks are two vast insulated columns of limestone, rising out of the sea, almost to a level with the precipitous cliffs which overlook them.

The Coast at Lydstep

Manorbier Castle

Their crannied sides and rough summits are in spring and early summer literally plastered with the white bodies of thousands of sea birds mostly "elligugs" (guillemots) and razorbills sitting on their eggs or young. From the cliff edges, arches, caverns and yawning crannies, characteristic of this weird coast, everywhere meet the eye, and occasionally a narrow bit of grassy slope squeezes sharply down between the heights and gives the visitor near access to the clear green Atlantic waters swinging into some cove below, where with reasonable luck he may see a seal or two disporting itself on the surface. Near the Stacks, too, is the Cauldron, a gigantic fissure in the surface of the hill. Looking down its precipitous sides as into some huge well, the sea may be seen boiling at its bottom 140 feet below, through an arched doorway. Northward again from here the eye ranges for miles along the rugged sea front towards the gentler coast line that opens out the wide mouth of Milford Haven with its island studded capes.

St. Govans Head, some four miles south of the Stacks, is approached through the hamlet of Bosherston and by the end of the lakes which for three winding miles so beautify Lord Cawdor's demesne of Stackpole. The same high, level, grass pastures edge the cliffs, which here continue their grim and awesome course. Generally precipitous, with their feet dipped deep in the churning sea, a gorge opens betimes, dropping down to a cove with perhaps a scrap of sandy beach. In one cleft near the fine headland of St. Govans, is strangely wedged a tiny medieval chapel of rude structure to which rough steps descend. Legend associates it with one of Arthur's knights, but it is actually dedicated to St. Cofe, the wife of a 6th century Welsh prince. A neighbouring ravine so nearly closes its two sides

PEMBROKE CASTLE.

at the seaward end as to suggest temptation to some reckless jumper. It is called " the huntsman's leap " from a tradition that a horseman once jumped the grim chasm, but was afterwards so terrified at the thought of his own performance that he died of fright! From St. Govans Head one looks eastward along a

Penally

Caldy Island and Coast near Penally

vista of grey limestone or red sandstone cliffs and headlands to the high green uplands and rugged sea walls and capes of Caldy island closing in the horizon.

Pembroke town is but some eight miles inland from here and is on the usual route from Tenby. All this region south of Milford Haven is in the Castle Martin division of the county, that village together with St. Twinnels, St. Petrox, Warren and others, raising characteristic church towers over the wide, treeless, verdant sweeps of, just here, large grass farms. The great historic castle of Pembroke obscures any slight interest that may attach to the old town beside it. It was one of the largest castles in Britain as befitted its importance to the realm. Originally but a rude fortress of the conquering Normans, it was re-built a century later, to be yet more enlarged with the passing years. Erected on a limestone ridge with almost precipitous sides, it is in great part surrounded by an inlet of the Haven, and when the tide is up the grey walls and towers are most effectively mirrored in its surface. Entered by an embattled gateway, the castle is still encircled by curtain walls strengthened by towers of which portions only remain. But the most striking feature is the round central keep of enormous thickness and 75 feet in height. A small fee secures entry to the castle through the great gateway into the spacious grassy enclosure, where with the handbook provided, the plan of the castle can be understood. It is now undergoing much needed repairs. Historically it is hallowed ground, so many great events have happened here. From its gates issued the great Earl Strongbow with the first Norman-Welsh conquerors of Ireland to take ship from the Haven. Henry II followed later. Other kings found temporary lodgement here, and here Henry VII with his Uncle Jasper, its Earl, spent his early days, to return again on his way to Bosworth field. Alone in south Wales, though nowadays but a country town, Pembroke stood for the Roundheads in the Civil War. Its mayor Poyer won deserved renown as its defender in a long siege, and then changing sides, justifiably as he thought, on Cromwell's accession to power, joined the Royalists in defying the Usurper himself till starved into surrendering Pembroke. He was executed, after drawing lots with three other leaders of this Welsh aftermath of the war.

HAVERFORDWEST.

Pembroke Dock is two miles distant, on the main Haven, with a population of some ten thousand, recently engaged in the naval works for building and repairing warships, that after more than a hundred years have been now permanently closed—a local disaster and present problem. Five miles down the Haven is Milford with its memories of Nelson and the Hamiltons, which suffered in the same way when displaced by Pembroke, but is now the centre of the largest fishery in south-west Wales. The Haven, some ten miles long below Pembroke Dock and as many more in its narrower ramifications up into the heart of the county, is one of the finest harbours in Europe. Hitherto naval men here stationed, almost alone among outsiders, have had knowledge of Pembrokeshire, and those of sporting or sociable tastes have always, I believe, thoroughly appreciated it. A regiment is still here, for no very obvious but doubtless sufficient reasons.

Across the water from Pembroke Dock a railway runs northward to Haverfordwest, the present county capital (6,000 population). Its castle, a huge four-sided pile with towers at two sides, dominates the town, which last rises sharply up from a narrow arm of the Haven formed by the western Cleddau where it meets the tide. The interior of the castle now fills the prosaic role of municipal offices. But of old it generally defied capture. Even Glyndwr and his French allies in 1405 could not take it, though they burned the town. It was built in the 12th century by Gilbert de Clare. Haverfordwest—why the later termination "west" no one knows—

was in the middle ages created a county of itself—within a county—and still remains so with full paraphernalia, carrying its double honours rather sadly perhaps nowadays as a mere farming centre. Still the town has always been of great importance in Pembrokeshire and before railways, when London was inaccessible, had its winter season to which the squires and their families resorted. On the river just below the town are the remains of an Augustinian priory of about 1200 date. Of the three town churches, St. Mary's, with much fine 13th century work, is the most interesting. This is the division of Rhoos, which is thought to have received more Flemish blood than other parts of south Pembrokeshire.

HAVERFORDWEST CASTLE.

Pembroke Castle, Western Tower

Haverfordwest

CHAPTER IV

CASTLES OF SOUTH PEMBROKESHIRE

TURNING towards Tenby again, and some three miles from Haverfordwest, stands the massive rectangular bulk of Picton castle. Though now occupied by the descendants of the Philipps family who acquired it in the 14th century, the necessary alterations have not seriously detracted from its medieval dignity, while the wooded park-lands picturesquely skirt the banks of a wandering fork of the wide branching Haven. In the adjoining grounds of Slebech Hall are the remains of a church of the Knights Templars who once owned the property. Five miles to the north-east is Llawhadden, one of the fortified palaces of the bishops of St. David's. A courtyard with towers at the angles inside a turreted gateway, survive. But the position of the castle, crowning a high hill above the wooded valley of the east Cleddau, is perhaps its greatest charm. The acquisitive Bishop Barlow who tore the lead roof off the palace at St. David's for his daughter's dower, played the same shabby trick here, while Cromwell himself who slept in the manor house completed the ruin. In the deep vale beneath, presenting an exquisite village scene, is the ancient parish church with its embattled tower.

Wiston and Narberth Castles in the same neighbourhood, both on the Anglo-Welsh frontier, are more ruinous and may be omitted. But to the southward, between Haverfordwest and Tenby, on the meadowy fringe of a straggling fork of Milford Haven, stands perhaps the most attractive of all the Pembrokeshire castles. This is Carew, a building that displays most effectively the adaptation of a medieval castle into a splendid Tudor residence, in this case inhabited till late in the 17th century. The original building passed, through Nesta, the beautiful daughter of Rhys ap Tudor, Prince of South Wales, to her husband, Gerald de Windsor, Constable of Pembroke, whose heirs took the name of Carew. The Carews owned the castle till the magnificent Rhys ap Thomas, Henry the Seventh's supporter already alluded to, acquired it together with many other estates. The castle will always be associated with the splendid fête held there by Sir Rhys, when a thousand guests and their retainers from all over Wales and the Border counties were magnificently entertained for a week with jousts and other sports, yet without a drop of blood being shed or even an angry word uttered! The castle ultimately passed back to the Carews, whose

PICTON CASTLE.

Carew Castle

Lamphey Palace Ruins

descendants now own it. The building is rectangular in shape with towers at the angles and gateway. The large late Tudor windows are a prominent feature. Its great size and entire detachment from all accessories on a clean water-fringed meadow add to its distinction. Near it is a richly ornamented Celtic cross 14 feet high, while the village church has a fine tower and contains some interesting effigies. Of the south Pembrokeshire castles that most call for notice within the limits of this booklet there only remains Lamphey, another fortified palace of the bishops of St. David's. This is within sight of Lamphey station between Pembroke and Tenby. With a foreground of meadows and background of lofty trees, Lamphey is a particularly serene and attractive spot, further embellished by the amenities of an adjoining country house and grounds. First erected in the 12th century, it was enlarged later by Bishop Gower, and ornamented with the same arcaded parapet as distinguishes his palace at St. David's. The shell of the building is of considerable size, and there is also a detached chapel extant with a good perpendicular window. Robert Devereux, Earl of Essex, Queen Elizabeth's favourite, spent his youth here. Hither, too, came Sir Rhys's splendid company from Carew castle to hear early mass.

As a last word on south Pembrokeshire, no one should fail to take a run along the Ridgeway, a road which rises to a high elevation at Penally near Tenby and maintains it as far as Lamphey, where it drops down into the Pembroke main road. It affords a beautiful bird's-eye view of the southern half of the county, with its mosaic of verdant grass farms, covering hill and dale, its white homesteads, its dominating church towers, interspersed with the rich woodland of many country seats, and always with the fine background to the northward of the Precelly mountains. Pembrokeshire scenery has a special quality, not easy to define, but it is not quite like any other county either in England or Wales. That there is always a flavour of Ireland about it is universally recognised, the better Ireland that is to say, while anyone who has hunted in the sister isle would recognise at once a similar country to Meath and Kildare—everywhere the same grass pastures with the same bank and ditch fences. But only Pembrokeshire sportsmen ride over them, and even they in declining numbers, from the increased cost of hunting and other difficulties. Fashion has never discovered them. Moreover the exotic sportsman could not get to London on off-days, or in frosty weather as is now the vogue!

St. David's Cathedral, Ruins of Bishop's Palace

St. David's Cathedral

CHAPTER V

ST. DAVID'S—THE VILLAGE CITY

ST. David's is still sixteen miles from a railway, but the adventures and delays of the old horse-stage from Haverfordwest, that used laboriously to negotiate its "seventeen hills" are now a thing of the past. The motor makes light of them and it is an interesting drive, more particularly as you approach St. Bride's bay, with Roch castle a mile inland, raising its single massive tower from the crag which lifts it up. Roch is on the Anglo-Welsh border and saw a great deal of fighting in olden times, but has been recently repaired and made habitable.

As you strike the top corner of St. Bride's bay, Newgale sands, with their strange pebble ridge, make a long break in the otherwise rugged coast. A pleasant place for a halt too is this, with a small house of entertainment to tempt one to linger over the fine prospect of the red cliffs and rocky islets that curve away towards St. David's. It is a strange country this last five miles of approach to the *Ultima Thule* of Welsh Christianity, something of a plateau, nearly bare of timber but everywhere a well-fenced region, of obviously good-sized farms, for the very scarcity of visible homesteads, which adds to its rather sad and windswept look. It is characteristic, too, of this country that isolated queer shaped hills should spring up inconsequently behind these smooth, lonely farming lands. Frequently too, the road drops into little ravines, carrying rivulets down to the neighbouring but invisible sea, and accounting for those many ascents and descents which were a proverbial joke with old travellers to St. David's. But Solva is much more than this. For here a full but narrow estuary pushes up a winding course between bold hills from the sea, and at its head, where the brook flows in and the St. David's road drops down to cross it, quite a large fishing village clusters. Besides the resident fishermen, it is a popular haunt, like many other of these coast villages, of the retired skipper, the master mariner, or of his family when he is still at sea.

RUINS OF ST. MARY'S COLLEGE AT ST. DAVID'S.

St. David's comes upon you almost unawares. You slip suddenly into an old-fashioned straggling village and catch sight of the top of a great weather-beaten tower rising behind it, apparently out of nowhere! This is the cathedral, which stands in a shallow valley just beneath the village. The descent to it lies through an embattled 13th-century gateway and down steps known as the "thirty-nine articles" into the wide spreading graveyard. Here rises the ancient fabric, its west end facing one in most imposing fashion, the more so for its situation of rural peace and seclusion, absolutely unique among British cathedrals. A stream murmurs beneath its walls and steals off through meadows to the sea a mile away. A few pleasant houses amid gardens and orchards stand informally on the hill slope, official residences, not in the least like the usual cathedral Close. First founded in the 6th century, of what like it was structurally when burned by the Danes in 1087, no one knows. Peter de Leia rebuilt it, but his tower fell on the building fifty years later. This necessitated re-construction of the choir and transept and the lower stages of the tower, while in 1300 the Lady chapel was added. Then came that great architect Bishop Gower, who raised both nave and tower, inserted decorated windows and added rood-screen and south porch. The beautiful roof of the nave, of Irish oak, is early 16th century, while about the same time the Lady chapel was vaulted by Bishop Vaughan, together with the chapel now bearing his name. During the Civil wars the leaden roof was stripped off the Lady chapel and presbytery aisles. Little was done till the 19th century when a great restoration was begun, which in detail was only recently completed. The exterior of the Cathedral is rather stern, as if in sympathy with the surrounding atmosphere. Most of it, save the west end (transition Norman), is in the Perpendicular style. The interior on the other hand is conspicuously ornate. The nave is Norman, and the local stone of which it is built shows varied and attractive colouring. The beautifully carved roof and Bishop Gower's rood-screen should be particularly noticed, also some quaint *miserere* stalls and the bishop's throne. The chapter house has been recently re-roofed and Edward the Second's chapel adjoining it restored and beautified. The lantern of the tower should also be noted for its beautiful proportions. The principal tombs are those of Edmund Tudor, father of Henry VII, of Bishop Gower and of Bishop Martyn, the builder of the Lady chapel. The supposed bones of St. David himself are treasured in a case. The saint was educated at this spot, then known as Menevia, founded a convent here, which gained a great reputation, and when the Archbishop of Caerleon, then Primate of Wales, resigned his see in favour of St. David, the latter shifted the seat of it to Menevia and died here in 601. Two pilgrimages to St. David's were regarded as the equivalent of one to Rome.

Close to the cathedral, on the north side are the lofty but ruinous remains of St. Mary's college, founded in 1365 by Bishop Houghton and John of Gaunt. But much the finest of these accessory buildings is the noble palace built by Bishop Gower in the 14th century. Its still ample ruins stand but a bow-shot from the west end and are slightly raised on the hill-slope beyond the stream, which prattles

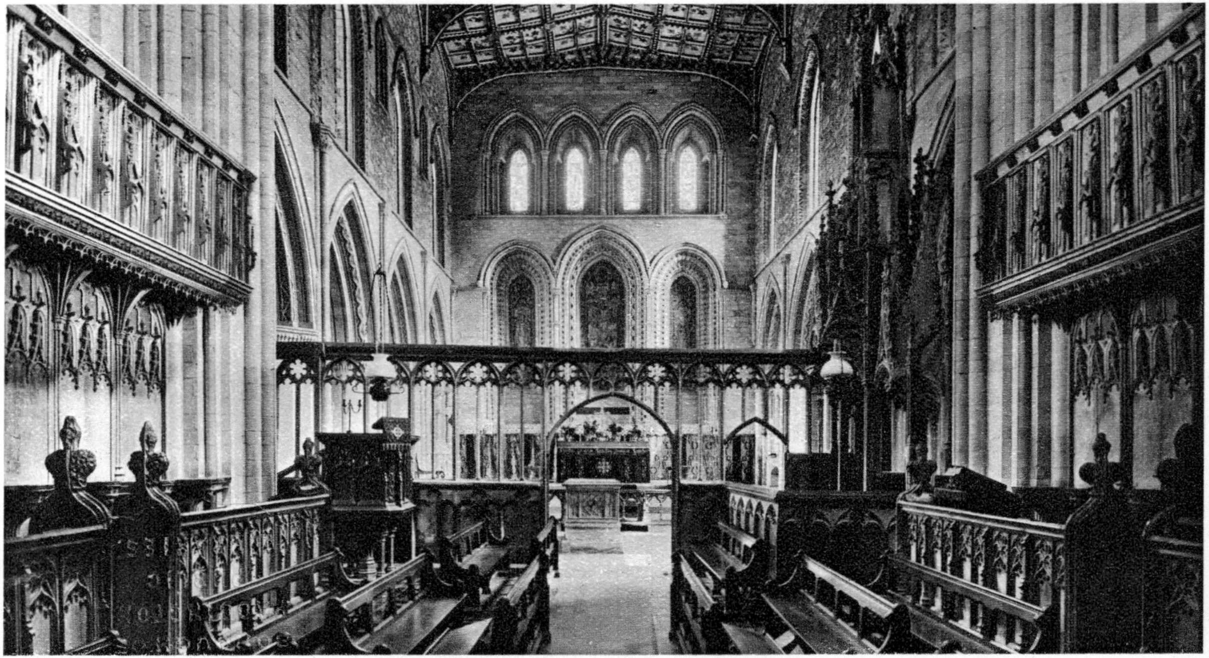

St. David's Cathedral, The Choir

Nun's Well Bay, near St. David's

beneath an old bridge and through a long meadow towards the sea. This was one of the finest buildings of its kind in the kingdom. Its great size was due to the profuse hospitalities incumbent upon the Prince bishop's position in such a remote spot. For kings and great barons with their large following came frequently to St. David's, sometimes on military, sometimes on religious errands and often en route for Ireland. Among these celebrities were William the Conqueror, Henry II and Edward I. Along the still lofty curtain walls that surround the large square, runs the elegant parapet arcade, that Bishop Gower repeated at Lamphey. Various buildings still in part survive within the Palace, including a smaller and a greater chapel. The large banquetting hall is still roof high and contains in its gable a perfect circular window.

The little "city," its legal definition, has not added to its population, about 1,500, or materially to its buildings within living memory, but grouped around its old market-cross, still breathes the very spirit of aloof and serene repose. While around it, on three sides, in wild weather the Atlantic booms on a stern and rugged shore. In August, however, its limited accommodation is fully bespoken. The beautiful cliff scenery, only interrupted by the welcome intrusion of Whitesand bay, with admirable sand dunes and golf course, is a great attraction. St. David's Head, Carn Lludi, two miles to the north is 600 feet high and carries both a camp, a cromlech, and remains of "round huts." Many old shrines and chapels, too, survive on this ever sacred shore. Caerfai bay, but a mile south, gives unsurpassed bathing, while the cliff scenery in all directions, diversified with the large island of Ramsey and its smaller satellites, delights the eye.

TREFFGARNE ROCKS.

Upper Solva

Lower Solva

CHAPTER VI

THE NORTH PEMBROKESHIRE COAST

IT is about 17 miles from St. David's to Goodwick and Fishguard, the main road running within two or three miles of the sea. The varied cliff scenery, however, is mostly concealed from the road traveller by the uplands that overhang it, till Strumble Head comes in sight, and that is magnificent. But no place of particular interest or beauty lies along this route. Still it is such a remote, wide-open farming country as to have a certain attraction in its very aloofness. From many hill summits on the road, spacious views open out over north Pembrokeshire, with its wonderful, varied colouring, grass prevailing but sprinkled about with patches of grain, heath and gorse-covered commons, upstanding crags, rounded hills or brown bogs. Always, too, comes the glint from far and near of the white farm houses. Within a few miles of Goodwick the great outstanding block of Pen Caer, of which Strumble Head is the crown and point, pushes the road behind it; the hills now mounting higher and the scenery becoming stern and wild. Before this diversion, however, at Abercastle near Mallery is one of the finest cromlechs in south Wales. It is impossible within our space here to attempt any serious mention of the great number of prehistoric remains within the district covered, but they are all given in detail by the many and excellent guide books.

A quite interesting approach to Goodwick and Fishguard by rail is from either Whitland or Haverfordwest (changing at Clarbeston Road). The railroad strikes the West Cleddau about five miles north of Haverfordwest at Treffgarne and thence more or less in company with the highway follows its picturesque course for a long way northward. The most interesting feature here is Treffgarne rocks, upstanding naked crags of almost mountainous appearance. They are part of the craggy ridge through which the West Cleddau cuts its way from the north. It was hereabouts that Owen Glyndwr was born. For though himself a north Wales magnate, his mother was a Pembrokeshire lady and gave birth to her redoubtable son while on a visit to her family. A farmhouse is doubtfully identified as the scene of an event (1350) so momentous to Wales. But an even more picturesque route to Fishguard is the alternative one by rail from Whitland, which branches off at Clynderwen and by a more northerly route passes through a section of the Precelly mountains and joins the twin line at Mathry Road station. The scenery here from Maenclochog to Puncheston is very fine indeed, the train climbing nearly 1,000 feet and descending through wild heathery heights from Rosebush station. The highest point of this fine group of hills, Precelly Top, or Foel-cwm-Cerwyn (1,750 feet), is just above the station. All around are wild hills from 1,500 to 1,600 feet, dipping at the east and the west to lower

Owen Glyndwr's Birthplace, Treffgarne

Fishguard Harbour

heights. The actual Precelly range is about ten miles long, approaching the sea near Newport and Fishguard bays on the west, but merging on the eastern or Carmarthenshire side into a country in itself so hilly as to make definition of limits difficult. But the visitor to Pembrokeshire should if possible

NEWPORT BAY.

climb the " Precelly Top " and yet more walk along the summit of the range from end to end. The view is magnificent, for not only the whole of Pembrokeshire is visible, but also the coast of Devon and even that of Ireland. While northward the Black mountains, the Plynlimon and Cader ranges and the whole of Cardigan bay to the furthest capes of Caernarvonshire can be seen in clear weather. Though the Precelly hills are not actually rugged in form, many of their summits and even ridges are capped with upstanding masses of crag, not unlike the Dartmoor tors : against the sky line the effect is most weird.

Fishguard is of course famous for its bay and harbour. The old town stands high up, overlooking the centre of the bay. Goodwick, which has grown vastly, lies in the south-western corner. The new docks stretch thence along the western side, while a breakwater runs laterally across the bay. Of the latter, the long, lofty headland of Dinas forms the eastern ; the great block of Pencaer, ending as mentioned in Strumble head, the western horn. From either at an elevation of some 500 feet the prospect of the great harbour is magnificent. Near Goodwick is the fine G.W.R. Fishguard Bay Hotel, with beautiful gardens spreading between the cliffs and sea. The Pencaer peninsula with its grand cliff scenery includes the old parish church of Llanwnda, of which Giraldus Cambrensis was rector, and several farms. The district is rich in prehistoric relics. It was at Carregwasted, a cove down below, that the French landed in February, 1797, some fifteen hundred strong, losing their guns in the process and being abandoned by their ships. It is a memorable story too long to tell here. But the invaders, after two days comparatively harmless occupation of the peninsula, seeing no hope of success, laid down their arms to some seven hundred Pembrokeshire yeomanry and militia who had gathered in a hurry to oppose them under Lord Cawdor, their acting Lord-Lieutenant. From Fishguard, a regular service of steamers to Ireland is maintained.

Behind Dinas head the bay of Newport opens, of much the same configuration but rather smaller than that of Fishguard. At its head stands the old town of Newport (2,000 population), which a small fishing industry, some summer visitors and retired skippers keep reasonably prosperous. Above it rises its ancient castle—the shell of two drum towers with

NEWPORT CASTLE.

a mansion attached. It was founded by the son of that Martin de Tours who, as already told, conquered northern, or Welsh, Pembroke under such favourable circumstances. Its owners still have the privilege of nominating the mayor of Newport, the present one, Sir Marteine Lloyd, being a lineal descendant of the founders, generally known as the "Lords of Kemys." Above the tower rises a pyramidical spur of the Precellys, Carnengli (1,150 feet), strikingly crowned by a mass of rocks which have forced their way through to the surface. Carn Engyl, "the hill of the angels," so called as the spot where St. Brynach, the founder of Christianity in this remote corner, sat in commune with the angels. The beautiful stream and deep, lovely valley of the Nevern opens out into Newport harbour. Nevern church, some way up its woody course, has great distinction, with its broad, massive Norman tower, pitch dark avenue of yew trees, and wonderful Celtic cross of St. Brynach, 12 feet high, before the porch. Within it on the window sills are some well known Ogham stones. It was re-founded by the conquering Martins, who there made their first headquarters. Higher up the valley is Henllys, where in a vanished house abode George Owen, also Lord of Kemys, or Cemmaes, successor and kin to the Norman family, who about 1600 wrote the most complete and intimate description of the Pembrokeshire of his day; the best Elizabethan work of its kind. An alternative route to the shorter sea coast road from Fishguard to Newport and Nevern is up the lovely valley of the Gwaen, which circles around by Llanllawer and Pontfaen behind the Carnengli group of hills, and thence descending the Clydach (12 miles). All the beauties of a Welsh mountain stream flowing under woody hills and by hamlets, old churches and "ancient things," cromlechs, crosses, maen heirion, and inscribed stones are here.

CELTIC CROSS IN NEVERN CHURCHYARD.

Fishguard, The Gwaun Valley

Newport Bay

CHAPTER VII

CARDIGANSHIRE AND TEIFYSIDE.

FROM Nevern the direct road northward to Cardigan (8 miles) climbs the high coast country which throws its bleak pasture farms up to the sky line, beneath which, unseen from the road, the dark rugged cliffs are battling with the sea. But the most profitable route to Cardigan is the circuit taken by the Western Welsh motor 'buses which, running high up the beautiful valley of the Nevern, turn north through Eglwyserw. A high country too is this and exposing glorious backward views of the long line of the Precelly mountains, with their strange caps of stone, and later on providing some rare peeps eastward over hills and dales into Carmarthenshire. The drive ends with a sharp descent to Cardigan and the vale of Teify, the county boundary here, and its embowering woods winding far beneath. All through northern Pembrokeshire Welsh is universally spoken, in the little towns, the villages, in the motor 'buses. The ancient tongue sounds strange filling the interior of an up-to-date motor 'bus!

I have brought the traveller into Cardiganshire by routes more or less in touch with the western coast. I must make space, however, to press an alternative upon him, if only for its extreme beauty. That is the line of railroad running up the Tâf valley from Whitland, crossing its high watershed over spurs of the Precellys and down through winding glens to Cardigan. The first stages from Whitland to Login, with the clear stream of the Tâf running a meadowy

NEVERN BRIDGE.

course in and out with the line is quite a good foretaste of what comes later as we mount into a still higher country by Llanfalted, Login and Llanglydwen. At Rhydowen the vale narrows, the streams of the Tâf get more turbulent, the high outliers of the Precellys show here and there above the nearer walls of the valley. At Llanfyrnach some lead and silver mine workings are a passing blemish on the charming scenery. At Crymmych the elevation is

Nevern

Cardigan, River Teify

800 feet and on either side Precelly flankers rise to 1,200 and 1,300 feet. Soon after this a long descent towards the Teify valley begins and opens out wide backward views over a glorious country to the whole range of the Precellys. The descent continues by glens and ravines and woods to Cardigan ; on the whole perhaps the most continuously picturesque two hours of railway travelling Pembrokeshire affords. The main highway from Narbeth northwards to Cardigan follows a rather more westerly and rather higher route through the same region.

Cardigan stands on the lower tidal reaches of the Teify, four miles from its mouth where at Gwbert-on-Sea a large hotel and golf links lend attraction to a fine rock-bound bay, with Cemmaes head on the one hand and the upstanding island of Cardigan on the other. The town itself save for a fine old bridge has no particular attraction. It is solid and reasonably thriving and just under 4,000 population. Hardly anything is left of the castle which played a stormy part in its day, while of the church, the chancel alone is old. A mile down the river at St. Dogmels, a large picturesque village, the fragments of its once important Benedictine abbey remain in the churchyard

CLIFFS AT GWBERT.

and vicarage grounds. There are some quaint old bits, too, in Cardigan itself, towards the river, survivals of the days when a brisk coasting trade flourished there.

But it will appeal to most visitors mainly as a convenient base for exploring a beautiful district, in which the ascent of the Teify valley takes the first place. Since the river is still tidal three miles up from Cardigan, a boat so far is advisable for viewing the ruins of the once mighty castle of Kilgerran, crowning a steep height above the river. Raised by an Earl of Pembroke on the site of a fortress of the Norman Clares, it was a scene of constant strife. Painted

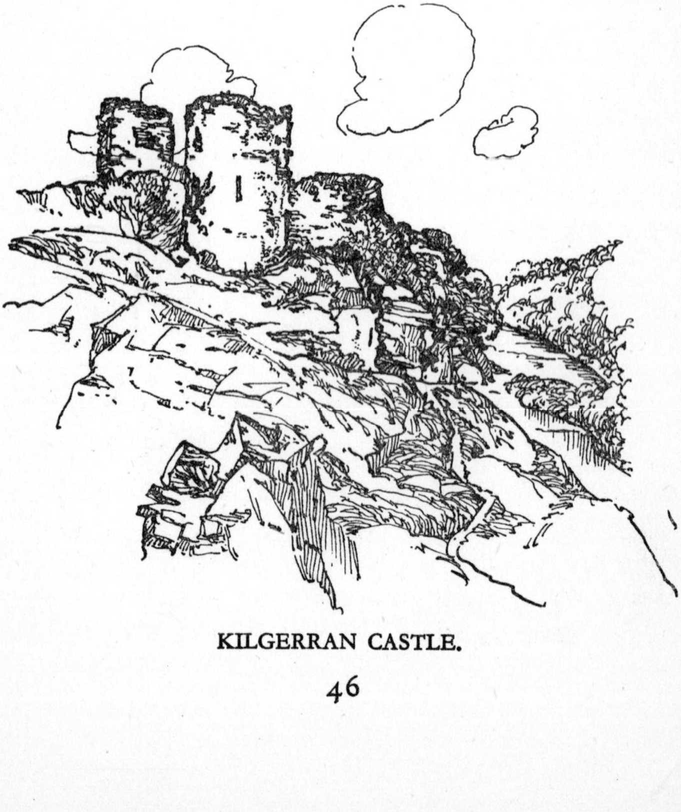

KILGERRAN CASTLE.

Newcastle Emlyn, Cenarth Bridge

Newcastle Emlyn, Castle Ruins

both by Turner and Wilson, its high perched hoary towers, looking down over mantling woods and winding waters, make the most imposing scene on all " Teivyside," as the Teify valley is affectionately called by its inhabitants. At Llechryd just above, a fine old bridge crosses the river, where its rapid waters meet the first sobering effects of the tide. Here the high road from Cardigan joins the river and follows it up to Newcastle Emlyn, about four miles on. Everywhere lovely reaches of the Teify, swirling from deep pools to glistening shallows, between red banks, amid meadows and hanging woods, delight the eye. This has been a famous salmon river for all time. Net fishers at the mouth and rod fishers above, here as elsewhere, wage their eternal struggle. It is also a first-class trout stream right up to its distant source among the mountains. Facilities for fishing vary according to district and must always be the subject of local enquiries. The motor 'buses of the Western Welsh Co., ply from Cardigan to Newcastle Emlyn, crossing over to the Carmarthenshire bank at Cenarth bridge, just below the rapids with which the river here runs down into a large salmon pool, where coracles may often be seen. From

NEWCASTLE EMLYN.

Newcastle Emlyn, a little town of 1,000 souls, a branch line of railroad joins the Aberystwyth-Lampeter-Carmarthen line at Pencader. The Teify at Newcastle Emlyn describes an extraordinary bend, almost encircling the high mound upon which the fragments of a once important castle occupy a still imposing site. Its crumbling walls, however, were actually raised by that potent Tudor gentleman, Sir Rhys ap Thomas of Carew castle. But long before his day Welsh princes and Norman lords waged furious wars around an earlier fortress. All the way up to Llandyssul, travelling either by rail or road, Teifyside retains its ever shifting charms of water, woodland, meadow and country seat. Its waters get more rapid, as in the woody gorges of Henllan and the rocky channels of Llandyssul, at which riverside village there is a good hotel and centre for anglers. Road and railway both leave the river here and run up the winding glen of the Tywelli brook to Pencader junction.

LLANDYSSUL.

We cannot here follow the Teify up its next stage of 14 miles to Lampeter. Llandyssul terminates what is generally known as Teifyside or Tivyside. The valley is not henceforward so strikingly beautiful as in its lower reaches. Lampeter with about 2,000 population is a pleasant rural little town, but better known as the seat of

Llandyssul

Lampeter College

the college so closely identified with the Welsh church. This last was built over a century ago round a quadrangle on the plan of an Oxford college. With its shady lawns and lying amid charming scenery, near the banks of the Teify, it is a most attractive spot. There are now about 160 undergraduates in residence, most, though not all, of whom take Holy Orders. Otherwise there is nothing of particular note at or around Lampeter, though there are many pleasant country houses with old traditions. The Assizes are now held here, having been removed from Cardigan as too remote. But hereabouts one comes into rather a different country, and I will ask the reader to take a glance at the map, when it will be seen that Cardiganshire is roughly the shape of a crescent moon, or let us say of a bent bow, with the string (not taut) representing the sea coast, and the bow, the mountainous back that it seems to turn towards the rest of Wales. The Teify follows the bow, approximately from its bottom point at Cardigan town right round to where, continuing the simile, the arrow point would rest. Lampeter is a little south of this line, but the Teify continues for another 20 miles, till at Strata Florida it turns right-handed into its mountain source.

CHAPTER VIII

SOUTH CARDIGANSHIRE

FOR most of this upper stage from Lampeter, the river skirts the foot of the mountain range that has for all time, though now modified by science, shut Cardiganshire off from the outer world and given it a character of its own, even in the Welsh world. This mountain wilderness, though it is not within our immediate subject, must be mentioned as it affects the whole of South Wales. It starts at the north with the Plynlimon mountains which are fairly well known to tourists. But from there it runs south for about 30 miles and in width from ten to twenty. An untrodden solitude, there are no roads through it. Practically no outsiders ever penetrate it or even know anything about it. It rises to 2,200 feet and is all wild mountain furrowed by many streams, sprinkled with a few tarns and occupied only by sheep and ponies. It is probably the largest solitude south of the Scottish Highlands. It contains bits of five counties, but strange to say has no collective name. The ancients called it the "mountains of Elynedd." From anywhere in Cardiganshire you may see its outer ramparts trailing along the sky line. Following up the Teify, ever and always a delightful stream, from Lampeter along

Lampeter

Strata Florida, Abbey Ruins

its fringes, its inner solitudes can be entered by farm tracks at Tregaron and Strata Florida, with stations on the Lampeter-Aberystwith line.

Taking Lampeter as the arrow head of the Cardiganshire bow, the arrow itself may aptly represent the vale of Aeron cutting across the county to the sea at Aberayron. Of that southern half of Cardiganshire included in "south-west Wales," the vale of Aeron is not only the choicest but the most easily explored portion. No frequenter of this charming vale

ABERAYRON.

can ever resist quoting the artless lines of some old-time bard printed by Sir S. Meyrick in his History of Cardiganshire, beginning:

"Sweet Aerons vale, unkown in song,
Demands the warbling lyre.
Shall silver Aeron glide along
And not a bard inspire?
What bard that Aeron sees can fail
To sing the charms of Aerons vale."

The G.W.R. runs a little branch line from Lampeter down the vale to Aberayron at its mouth. Some four miles west of Lampeter both rail and road drop sharply down to the vale. The Aeron just here has run down from the northward for some ten miles out of Llyn Eiddwen, a lake in the Mynydd Bach hills which gives it birth. On its downward course the stream has passed many secluded churches and villages. Among them Llangeitho is particularly picturesque, but has some further interest as containing the old chapel erected for Daniel Rowlands, once vicar of the parish. Rowlands was one of the band of churchmen in the early 19th century who adopted Methodism and took whole congregations out of the Church by their impassioned vehemence. He was regarded as the best preacher of his day and thousands from all parts flocked to his chapel at Llangeitho. His unfortunate successor to the parish church was left to read the services "to his sister"! A statue of the eloquent Calvinist looks down from his chapel precincts upon the passer-by. But where the traveller from Lampeter meets the vale five miles below is from a height above it whence the prospect down its course towards the sea overlooks a beautiful mass of wooded hills ; while here and there towering above them to a thousand or more feet is one of those wild and inconsequent heights that the broken surface of the " sweet shire of Cardigan " flings heavenward. The way drops down into Llanfihangel Ystrad, where beside the ancient church an old gentleman, one John Davies, who died in 1799, proclaims himself upon his tomb,

" Cordwainer, scribe, musician,
Poet sublime in blank or rhyme,
Divine and politician."

At Talsarn, a mile off the road, is some quaint cottage architecture of the south-west Wales type with the braided thatch roof. In the grounds of Llanlear, one of the seats of the Lewes family, of old name in the vale, was once a monastery of White nuns of which traces remain. Fine trees, too, just here overhang the road, not always oaks, so common in Wales, but often ash trees of giant proportions, while at the manor of Green Grove some splendid fir trees stand between road and river. High wooded hills shut in the vale and the Aeron sparkles around their feet in its alder-shaded bed. Below Green Grove the valley widens again and Trycrug mountain rises above it to 1,100 feet. The mansions of Ty-glyn and Ty-glyn-aeron amid their embowering woods and green pastures add to the charm of the scene. Attached to the former house is an ancient chapel dedicated curiously enough to St. Alban. On its gable end is a long-silent old clock by whose deep voice, says Miss Evelyn Lewes in her compact little "Guide to the Aeron Valley," booming over the valley, people used to set their watches. As you draw towards Aberayron, the hills meeting in V-shape with the tall church spire rising in the centre and the line of the sea behind, make a composition once seen is not readily forgotten. The road thither runs for some distance through the magnificent arches of the Hengeraint oaks. Near the river and under the hill is the quaint little church of Llanerchayron. This is dedicated to St. Non, a saint we have never encounted before either in Wales or England. A monumental cross outside the door commemorates Mrs. Lewes of Llanayron House close by and lady of the manor, who died in her 104th year. Aberayron has some 1,300 inhabitants. How many of these are retired sea captains and their families we do not know. But it is commonly said that Cardiganshire, though not greatly given to fishing enterprise has more captains and mates sailing "the seven seas" than any other county in Britain, though Pembrokeshire cannot be far behind. These little coast towns consequently contain all kinds of unsuspected curiosities from various parts of the world and unsuspected quiet folk, including wives, who have seen countries that the fashionable "Globe-trotter" rarely looks upon. Like all these little seaports turned into modest summer resorts, Aberayron has had its day of ship-building and trading but now regards the summer visitor as its chief asset. It is more attractive perhaps at the back than in the front! Its pier and harbour were made as far back as 1807.

Aberayron, River Ayron

Tresaith

It is a beautiful motor-'bus run from here along the coast (more or less) to Cardigan, particularly the first part of it to New Quay—smaller than Aberayron, and more picturesque, with its curving sandy bay, outstanding headlands and pretty setting of the village on the slope of a hill amid abundant foliage. Near it, too, the road winds through beautiful leafy dingles watered by tumbling streams. Set in one of these on its descent to the sea and near the road is the ancient manor house of Wern Newydd, now a farm house. In 1485 its then owner, Eimon ap Dafydd Llwyd or Lloyd, entertained Henry VII as he passed through here on his way to Bosworth. The present occupants are always ready to show visitors, not only the room, but the bed in which the king slept! After New Quay the Cardigan road turns upward and inland, passing the old Synod inn, a landmark of ancient note at four cross roads. Thence it runs mainly along the high country looking down on those gaps in the coast where lie in their order the little ports of Llangranog, Penbryn, Tresaith, and Aberporth. The views eastward and inland over Cardiganshire, with its chequered farming lands and upspringing heights, are nearly always of wide extent, backed by the long line of mountains already described as bounding the county. Each of the coast villages above mentioned sends a road up to meet the highway and the motor 'buses. They are all within an easy walk of the latter and well worth a visit.

As a last word, the drive by motor 'bus from Cardigan and Newcastle Emlyn to Carmarthen should, if possible, not be omitted. It crosses the high country south of the Teify valley and strikes the lovely valley of the Gwili above Conwil, and thence down to Carmarthen through some enchanting valley scenery.

END.

New Quay

Fishguard Bay Hotel, Goodwick (Pemb.)